ARE YOU

Afraid YET?

The Science Behind

SCARY STUFF

For Donna, my candle in the dark, and Daisy, my little devil dog — S.J.O.

For my parents, Joe and Sheila Kaposy — J.K.

Kids Can Press acknowledges the financial support of the Government of Ontario, through the Ontario Media Development Corporation's Ontario Book Initiative; the Ontario Arts Council; the Canada Council for the Arts; and the Government of Canada, through the BPIDP, for our publishing activity.

Published in Canada by
Kids Can Press Ltd.
25 Dockside Drive
Toronto, ON M5A 0B5

Published in the U.S. by
Kids Can Press Ltd.
2250 Military Road
Tonawanda, NY 14150

www.kidscanpress.com

Edited by Valerie Wyatt
Designed by Marie Bartholomew

The paper used to print this book was produced with elemental chlorine-free pulp harvested from managed sustainable forests.

The hardcover edition of this book is smyth sewn casebound.
The paperback edition of this book is limp sewn with a drawn-on cover.
Manufactured in Singapore, in 1/2011 by Tien Wah Press (Pte) Ltd.

CM 09   0 9 8 7 6 5 4 3
CM PA 09   0 9 8 7 6 5 4 3 2

Library and Archives Canada Cataloguing in Publication

O'Meara, Stephen James, 1956–
     Are you afraid yet? : the science behind scary stuff / written by Stephen James O'Meara ; illustrated by Jeremy Kaposy.

ISBN 978-1-55453-294-0 (bound)
ISBN 978-1-55453-295-7 (pbk.)

1. Monsters—Miscellanea—Juvenile literature.
2. Science—Juvenile literature. I. Kaposy, Jeremy
II. Title.

BF1566.O44 2009   j001.944   C2008-903251-9

Kids Can Press is a Corus™ Entertainment company

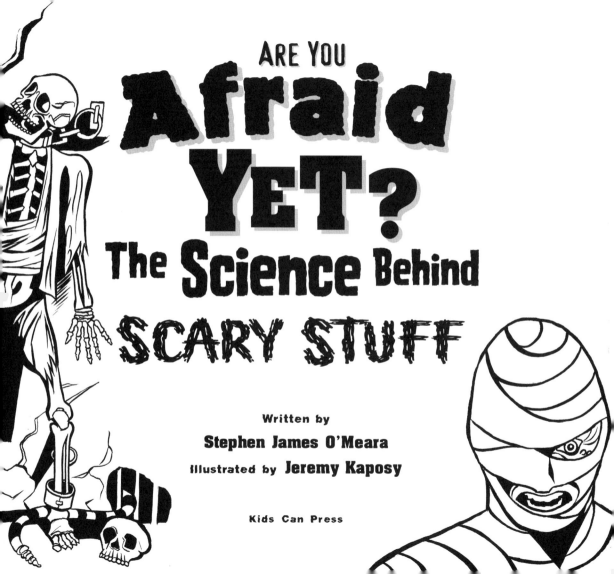

ARE YOU

Afraid YET?

The Science Behind

SCARY STUFF

Written by
Stephen James O'Meara
Illustrated by **Jeremy Kaposy**

Kids Can Press

HAVE A SAFE FRIGHT!

SCREAM! GO AHEAD AND SCREAM! AND PUT SOME TONSIL INTO IT!

I'M STEVE O'MEARA, AND I'LL BE YOUR GUIDE THROUGH 80 PAGES OF MURDER, MAYHEM AND MAGGOTS.

Fear is the oldest and most powerful emotion. We're born with fears. We learn new fears. And we spend much of our lives trying to overcome them.

That's why some scientists dedicate their lives to studying fear. They're dying to understand how a chemical reaction races through the brain and body causing us to feel afraid.

"Fear central," they know, is the amygdala, located deep at the base of the brain.

This almond-sized gob of neurons stores memories, recalls past experiences and alerts us to threats. It's the brain's terror alarm. Once the amygdala detects danger, it sends chemical signals to other parts of the brain that prepare the body for a response — usually to fight or flee.

By getting a grip on fear, scientists hope to help the millions of people around the globe who suffer from chronic anxiety disorders, such as panic attacks.

Amazingly, a little bit of fear may be good for you — especially in the safety of a movie theater or amusement park. By facing fear over and over again, you learn how to keep your cool when stressed. So bring on that scary movie and step into that roller coaster. And don't be afraid to be afraid.

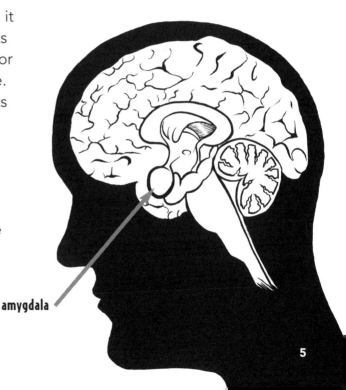

amygdala

THE MIRROR IN THE Mind

Why do our spines tingle when we read a horror tale or watch a scary movie? Why does our skin crawl when we see someone about to walk into a giant spider web? Meet the mirror neurons. These special brain cells fire up whenever we see, hear or read something that has made us afraid in the past. The neurons use that information to figure out what's likely to come next. It's all about anticipating danger, so we can avoid it.

MIRROR **MIRROR** IN THE **MIND**.

YOU NEURON!

Giacomo Rizzolatti, the Italian neuroscientist who led the team that discovered mirror neurons, says our survival depends on them. By allowing us to share in someone else's fear or feel their pain, we are brought closer together. (Just imagine if you *didn't* have this ability — you wouldn't much care what happened to others.)

But that's not all. Mirror neurons help our brains analyze scenes to detect danger. When we hear that scary *dum-dum-dum-dum* music from the movie *Jaws*, our minds scream, "SHARK!"

Mirror neurons also help us guess the intentions of others. So when we see ol' Leatherface pull the cord on his chainsaw, we can be pretty sure he's not heading out to trim a tree.

The Galloping Ghost!

WHAT GOES, "CLIPPITY CLOP, CLIPPITY CLOP ... PLOP!?" IT'S THE HEADLESS HORSEMAN OF SLEEPY HOLLOW — LOSING HIS HEAD.

ACTUALLY, IN WASHINGTON IRVING'S CLASSIC TALE "THE LEGEND OF SLEEPY HOLLOW," IT'S A GANGLY SCHOOLMASTER NAMED ICHABOD CRANE WHO "LOSES IT." IT HAPPENS AT MIDNIGHT, ON AN OLD WOODEN BRIDGE OVER A HAUNTED STREAM. AS ICHABOD TRIES TO GET HIS FEARFUL HORSE OVER THE BRIDGE, HE COMES FACE TO FACE WITH WHAT HE BELIEVES IS THE HEADLESS HORSEMAN. TERROR GRIPS ICHABOD'S HEART.

FOLLOW ALONG NOW AS WASHINGTON IRVING DESCRIBES WHAT HAPPENS TO ICHABOD'S BODY AS FEAR TAKES OVER. AND CHECK OUT THE SCIENTIFIC EXPLANATION OF WHY ICHABOD'S BODY RESPONDS TO FEAR IN THE WAY IT DOES.

SUDDENLY [ICHABOD] HEARD A GROAN — HIS TEETH CHATTERED AND HIS KNEES SMOTE AGAINST THE SADDLE.

WHEN WE GET SCARED, OUR BRAIN ORDERS THE RELEASE OF ADRENALINE AND A FLOOD OF OTHER HORMONES (CHEMICAL MESSENGERS) INTO THE BLOODSTREAM. INSTANTLY, THE BODY IS READY TO FIGHT OR FLEE.

WHEN AFRAID, OUR PULSE INCREASES. OUR HEARTS GO FROM PUMPING ABOUT 4 L (1 GAL.) OF BLOOD PER MINUTE TO 19 L (5 GAL.).

AS HE APPROACHED THE STREAM, HIS HEART BEGAN TO THUMP.

IN THE DARK SHADOW OF THE GROVE ... HE BEHELD SOMETHING HUGE ... LIKE SOME GIGANTIC MONSTER READY TO SPRING UPON THE TRAVELER.

AFRAID IN THE DARK, OUR SENSES SHARPEN. OUR PUPILS DILATE, LETTING MORE LIGHT IN. OUR ABILITY TO DETECT MOTION INCREASES. INDISTINCT SHAPES OPEN THE DOOR TO THE IMAGINATION.

WHEN FEAR TIGHTENS THE TINY MUSCLES ATTACHED TO EACH HAIR, THEY TENSE, MAKING THE HAIRS STAND UPRIGHT. THIS TRAPS AIR AND INSULATES THE SKIN. IT ALSO MAKES US MORE SENSITIVE TO OUR SURROUNDINGS.

THE HAIR OF THE AFFRIGHTED PEDAGOGUE ROSE UPON HIS HEAD WITH TERROR.

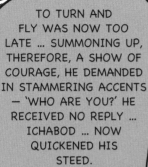

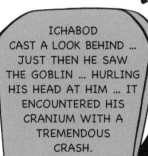

Speaking of **KEEPING** Your **HEAD** ...

It's been called the "blade" and the "widow maker." But its real name is the guillotine — a decapitation machine that put an end to executioners' complaints about dull swords, loose nooses and messy mutilations.

Head-lopping contraptions have been around for more than 700 years, but the most famous was *la guillotine* — a real crowd-pleaser in France in the late 1700s. It had a heavy, angled blade that slid on rails between two wooden uprights nearly 4.5 m (15 ft.) tall. Before the count of one (0.75 seconds, to be precise), the victim's head would fly into a bucket. **SWIIISH!** ... A basket every time!

FREAKY FACTS

◊ When a person is beheaded, the brain is severed from the spinal cord and the victim bleeds to death.

◊ After decapitation, blood squirts from the neck's severed veins and arteries. The heart continues to pump blood for a few minutes.

◊ A pumping heart has enough pressure to blast blood 9 m (30 ft.) into the air.

◊ Massachusetts cardiologist Mario Motta says that if you "surgically cut off a head and connect all arteries to veins carefully," the heart will continue to beat for up to ten minutes.

◊ Once blood flow to the brain stops, neurons become deprived of oxygen. All electrical activity ceases, and biological death occurs.

The Staring Eyes!

IN 1905, A FRENCH DOCTOR NAMED BEAURIEUX WATCHED THE GUILLOTINED HEAD OF HENRI LANGUILLE AS THE EYELIDS AND LIPS "WORKED IN IRREGULARLY RHYTHMIC CONTRACTIONS FOR ABOUT FIVE OR SIX SECONDS."

DR. BEAURIEUX THEN SHOUTED "LANGUILLE!" AND SAW THE MAN'S EYELIDS SLOWLY LIFT UP, "SUCH AS HAPPENS IN EVERYDAY LIFE, WITH PEOPLE AWAKENED OR TORN FROM THEIR THOUGHTS."

DR. BEAURIEUX SHOUTED THE CRIMINAL'S NAME AGAIN. AGAIN LANGUILLE'S EYELIDS LIFTED. BUT THIS TIME, "UNDENIABLY LIVING EYES FIXED THEMSELVES" ON THE DOCTOR.

THE SEVERED HEAD

In 1886, after experimenting with the freshly severed head of a criminal, two British researchers, Regnard and Loye, found that "not a trace of consciousness remains two seconds after beheading."

What do scientists believe today? Is a severed head aware of its situation? Florida pathologist Ron Wright says it is probably safe to say that a guillotined head remains conscious for about thirteen seconds — long enough to figure out that it is not attached to its body. Other scientists estimate an awareness time of somewhere between five and twenty seconds.

It may also be possible for a severed head to be aware long enough to blink once for "no" and twice for "yes" in response to a question, as has been observed in the past.

Awareness stops once the brain's high-energy phosphates, which energize the cells that keep the brain going, run out of "gas" (oxygen and sugar). How long that takes may depend on the victim's physique and health.

TRUTH OR Scare

Try to sink your fangs into this one, my friends. A man reaches down to a rattlesnake he's just decapitated. Suddenly, the severed snake head lunges and bites the man.

Well, sometimes truth is scarier than fiction because — news flash! — snake heads *can* bite after death. In fact, studies have shown that a severed rattlesnake head will try to attack objects waved in front of it for up to *an hour* after death.

In 1999, Joseph Slowinski, a herpetologist at the California Academy of Sciences in San Francisco, told *New Scientist* magazine that the biting might be a reflex action triggered by infrared sensors in the snake's pit organ. This is a structure between the snake's nostril and eye that detects body heat.

The lesson: If you see a dead rattler, let it rest in peace.

FREAKY FACTS

◗ Dr. Joseph B. Slowinski died in 2001 at age 38 from a highly venomous snake bite while conducting scientific research in Myanmar (Burma).

Mike, the Headless Chicken

The next time someone says, "Stop running around like a chicken with its head cut off," tell them about Mike, the Headless Chicken of Fruita, Colorado. Actually Mike was a rooster who was beheaded on September 10, 1945. But when the axe fell it missed Mike's jugular vein. Blood clots sealed up the neck wound and kept the bird's circulatory system intact.

The axe also missed one ear and the brain stem, so the bird retained all its reflex actions and could hear. In fact, "Miracle Mike" showed no signs of suffering and continued to act like a normal rooster, gurgling out a crowlike sound and trying to preen its feathers.

Lloyd Olsen kept Mike alive by using an eyedropper to feed the bird through its open esophagus. Mike died in an unfortunate choking accident in March 1947. By then, he had lived for eighteen months without a head.

The RETURN of Frankenstein

He's giant. He's stiff. He's made out of parts from different corpses. And he's been shocked to life with electricity. He's Frankenstein's monster, and since his 1931 film debut, he's become the poster child of classic horror.

Aside from his mirror-cracking looks, what frightens us most is his fragile state of mind. The monster wants to be loved, but if anyone looks at him and screams (and everyone does), this big softy suddenly goes berserk. He throws his creator off a windmill and even drowns a little girl, although that was an accident.

FRANKENSTEIN REMINDS US THAT FEAR INCREASES WHEN WE FACE THE UNPREDICTABLE OR UNCONTROLLABLE. IF YOU KNOW SOMEONE WHO CAN BLOW A NECK BOLT AT THE DROP OF A HAT, YOU'LL UNDERSTAND WHY FRANKENSTEIN'S MONSTER CONTINUES TO UNNERVE US.

"Crazy, AM I?"

Long before Frankenstein appeared in the movies, he was the star of a book written in 1818 by a young woman named Mary Shelley. Shelley wanted you to fear not so much the monster as the monster's creator, Victor Frankenstein, who uses science to experiment with life without considering the consequences. Her tale was inspired by accounts of 19th-century experimenters using electricity to animate corpses.

Today, doctors mimic Dr. Frankenstein, but for good rather than evil. They routinely harvest live organs from the dead, keep them fresh on ice and then transplant them into other bodies. They also install mechanical bits and pieces into humans. Heart surgeons keep patients alive with heart–lung machines, pacemakers and artificial hearts. Amputees get artificial limbs, the hearing impaired have cochlear implants, and artificial skin offers hope to burn victims.

Countless people benefit from procedures that would once have been considered **FREAKISH**. But where do we draw the line with science? What is acceptable science?

TRUTH OR Scare

In the late 1960s and early '70s, Dr. Robert White, a neurosurgeon in Cleveland, Ohio, went one step further. He stitched the **SEVERED** heads of monkeys onto fresh corpses of other headless monkeys, then brought the animals back to life. When one monkey regained consciousness, it attempted to bite the finger of one of White's assistants.

Was White a crazed monster? Not if you believe, as some doctors do, that a head transplant could one day save or extend the life of a quadriplegic. A quadriplegic's body is paralyzed from the neck down, but everything from the neck up functions. The body's organs, however, usually give out more quickly than normal. Transplanting a quadriplegic's head onto another body could extend his or her life by a decade or more.

THE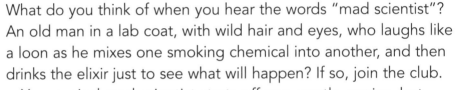

What do you think of when you hear the words "mad scientist"? An old man in a lab coat, with wild hair and eyes, who laughs like a loon as he mixes one smoking chemical into another, and then drinks the elixir just to see what will happen? If so, join the club.

Your typical mad scientist starts off as a gentle genius, but then it's all down hill. Some become obsessed with sinister tasks. They create bizarre machines, such as death rays, to destroy the world. Others turn humans into horrifying beasts. Then there are those who experiment on themselves, using drugs or elixirs to gain new powers.

In 1886, Robert Louis Stevenson wrote the classic mad scientist story in his chilling book *The Strange Case of Dr. Jekyll and Mr. Hyde*. To this day, some members of the American Psychiatric Association recommend the book as a useful primer on **DRUG ABUSE**.

IN THE BOOK, A KINDLY DR. JEKYLL EXPERIMENTS WITH A MIND-ALTERING DRUG THAT TURNS HIM INTO THE EVIL MR. HYDE. DAY BY DAY, DR. JEKYLL GROWS MORE DEPENDENT ON THE CHEMICAL. FINALLY, IT DESTROYS HIM.

I WAS SLOWLY LOSING HOLD OF MY ORIGINAL AND BETTER SELF, AND BECOMING SLOWLY INCORPORATED WITH MY SECOND AND WORSE.

OUR MENTAL STATE DEPENDS ON ONLY A FEW THOUSAND NEURONS IN THE BRAIN'S HYPOTHALAMUS. THIS SMALL, CONE-SHAPED STRUCTURE IN THE MIDDLE OF THE BRAIN REGULATES, AMONG MANY OTHER THINGS, OUR BEHAVIOR. "DRUGS," SAYS MINNESOTA PSYCHIATRIST WILLIAM SHEEHAN, "CAN HIJACK THE HYPOTHALAMUS'S ELECTRICAL AND CHEMICAL MACHINERY AND CHANGE ONE'S PERSONALITY. THEY CAN ARTIFICIALLY PRODUCE TEMPORARY STATES OF ECSTASY, FEELINGS OF SUPERHUMAN STRENGTH, DEPRESSION OR PARANOIA. A DRUG MAY TURN A MANIACAL MURDERER INTO A DOCILE SHEEP OR A MILD-MANNERED PERSON INTO A MANIACAL MURDERER."

THE CASE of the Invisible PARENTS

Children need their parents to survive. That's why they sometimes cling to them. That may also be why parents play peekaboo — to get the child used to the idea that parents sometimes "disappear" for a while.

But what if your parents (or friends) really did vanish. In fact, what if they could vanish whenever they wanted to? Would that be cool or **DEEPLY CREEPY?** Read on to find out.

OUT OF Sight!

In H.G. Wells's 1897 book *The Invisible Man*, an obsessed scientist, Jack Griffin, discovers the secret of invisibility.

VISIBILITY DEPENDS ON THE WAY LIGHT INTERACTS WITH A BODY. A BODY CAN ABSORB, REFLECT OR BEND LIGHT, OR IT CAN DO ALL THESE THINGS. IF IT DOESN'T, WE CANNOT SEE THE BODY.

GRIFFIN CONCOCTS A FORMULA THAT MAKES HIM INVISIBLE. FEELING ALL-POWERFUL (AND IMPOSSIBLE TO SEE), THE INVISIBLE MAN STARTS A REIGN OF TERROR. BUT THE EXPERIMENT BACKFIRES. GRIFFIN LOSES HIS MIND AND THEN HIS LIFE, TAKING THE SECRET OF INVISIBILITY WITH HIM TO THE GRAVE. OR DID HE?

TRUTH OR Scare

Think invisibility is fantasy? Well, in 2006, scientists at Duke University in North Carolina, the Imperial College London and the San Diego–based company SensorMetrix created the first "invisibility cloak."

The new technology relies on materials that can bend light around objects, like water flowing around a pebble, and erase shadows so it looks like nothing is there.

But before you get too excited … The cloaking device measures only 12 cm (5 in.) wide and 2.5 cm (1 in.) tall. And it works only with microwaves, not visible light. Researchers believe a Harry Potter–style invisibility cloak may materialize — or dematerialize — in a few decades. (Let's just hope it doesn't get into the wrong hands.) Still, scientists are one step closer to achieving … absolutely nothing.

Hidden Horrors!

Have you ever put your hand in a dark hole or corner and touched something unexpected? Have you ever been treading water when something suddenly brushed past your foot?

There's nothing more frightening than the unseen coupled with the unknown.

A hundred or so years ago, scientists had to face these fears as they penetrated uncharted corners of the world and explored dark jungles, isolated islands and the watery depths. What unseen horrors might await them, they wondered? Could exotic life forms, such as prehistoric beasts, still roam the Earth?

By the 1930s, most of the world's dark corners had been explored. Fantasies about lost worlds started to die out. But films like *King Kong* and *The Creature from the Black Lagoon* (the retold story of Kong in a marine setting) kept the **FEAR** of the unknown alive — at least at local movie theaters.

Long LIVE Kong?

King Kong, the Eighth Wonder of the World, was a fictitious 15 m (50 ft.) tall mountain gorilla that lived on Skull Island in the remote South Pacific. Kong shared this lost world with huge dinosaurs, such as Allosaurus and Stegosaurus.

How could all these massive creatures survive on one small island?

They couldn't, according to the theory of island biogeography. On small islands, food is scarce and space limited, so big beasts like Kong would either have to get off the island or die off. And since Kong and his king-sized friends couldn't swim or fly …

MONSTER MATH!

When it comes to monsters, size matters. Take Kong, for example. He's a Hollywood gorilla that's ten times the normal size. But the beast's shape hasn't changed, and that's a giant mistake made by the movie's creators. The late biologist John Haldane said it best in his 1928 essay "On Being the Right Size." He said: "At ten times a gorilla's normal height, King Kong would be 1000 times heavier. To support this huge weight, Kong's shape should have changed — his legs would have to be much shorter and thicker. Otherwise, the force on his bones would be too great and they would break into smithereens."

Yes, Kong's bones would have crumbled under his ferocious weight.

> FOR EVERY TYPE OF ANIMAL THERE IS A MOST CONVENIENT SIZE, AND A LARGE CHANGE IN SIZE INEVITABLY CARRIES WITH IT A CHANGE IN FORM.

FREAKY FACTS

♦ In the original 1933 movie, King Kong is about 6 m (20 ft.) tall at the beginning of the movie but ends up about 15 m (50 ft.) by the end. Whoops!

Bigfoot Stinks

A giant creature the size and shape of King Kong can't exist. But some people insist that a big and mysterious apeman does. Yes, it's Sasquatch (affectionately known as Bigfoot). This fuzzy forest freak walks on two legs, swings long, monkey-like arms and smells like a skunk on fire.

Sure, some grainy photos of Bigfoot exist. But that Bigfoot turned out to be a man in a monkey suit. And sure, there have been Bigfoot footprints, loose hair, blood and (ahem!) droppings. Skeptical research scientists, however, have found that the footprints are the product of pranksters wearing fake feet, the blood is

transmission fluid and the feces belong to known animals. And the hair? Most hair samples either belong to other animals or are fake fibers. It's true that some hairs have not yet been identified. But inconclusive evidence is not positive proof of a claim.

That said … absence of evidence is not necessarily evidence of absence.

In 1935, fossils of a giant ape called Gigantopithecus were found in China and parts of Southeast Asia. The creature stood about 3 m (10 ft.) tall — the same height as Bigfoot. Gigantopithecus might have died off as recently as 100 000 years ago.

Could Bigfoot be a modern relative of Gigantopithecus?

It's possible. But, considering the lack of physical evidence, it's likely that Bigfoot doesn't exist. The big question is why hasn't one of the countless thousands of Bigfoots that have been sighted ever left a body behind — say, after being hit by an SUV or dropping dead from a **HEART ATTACK**? Until a body turns up, Bigfoot will remain a living legend to those who want to believe in it and a nagging mystery for the skeptics to solve.

Now Fear THIS!

Forget Kong. The most terrifying jungle monsters are so small that billions of them could fit inside a drop of blood. We're talking about "hot agents" — killer viruses, many of which lurk in the world's rain forests. These viruses will not emerge until humans enter their ecosystems and become infected.

What happens to an infected person? One such killer virus — Ebola — eats its human host. First the infected person begins to vomit blood. Then his bowels burst. His other internal organs turn into a hot viral soup. As the human host dies, the infected fluid oozes out of every orifice in search of a new host. Like a lost child, a virus cannot survive on its own. Like a pirate, it continually "jumps ship," taking over, then destroying, its new host.

THERE'S BAD NEWS AND THEN THERE'S MORE BAD NEWS. EBOLA IS ONE OF ABOUT 150 VIRUSES KNOWN TO INFECT PEOPLE, AND MORE ARE JUST WAITING TO BE DISCOVERED. SOME COULD TRIGGER HORRIBLE INFECTIONS THAT COULD LEAD TO GROTESQUE DEATHS. ALL THESE VIRUSES ARE WAITING FOR IS YOU TO INVADE THEIR ENVIRONMENT. DO YOU DARE?

You Monster!!!!

Let's face it — most monsters have looks that only a mother could love. Their faces and bodies are contorted and deformed. In his 1831 classic tale *The Hunchback of Notre Dame*, Victor Hugo gave monster characteristics similar to a human being. The result was Quasimodo.

AN ENORMOUS HUMP ROSE BETWEEN HIS SHOULDERS, AND HIS LEGS WERE SO WARPED THAT HIS KNEES TOUCHED.

HIS BODY WAS A "TWISTED GRIMACE," AND STIFF RED HAIR BRISTLED FROM HIS HUGE HEAD.

HIS HANDS AND FEET WERE ENORMOUS, MONSTROUS. HE LOOKED "LIKE A GIANT WHO HAD BEEN BROKEN INTO PIECES AND HAPHAZARDLY PUT BACK TOGETHER AGAIN."

WOMEN WHO SAW QUASIMODO COVERED THEIR FACES IN HORROR!

33

Monster UGLY!

What is ugly? What is beautiful?

Many scientific studies have shown that we consider people beautiful when their faces and bodies are symmetrical — the same on both sides. Studies have also shown that faces with childlike features — small jaws, small noses, large eyes and defined cheekbones — rate high on the beauty scale. Toss in smooth skin and shiny hair and voila! You've got the looks.

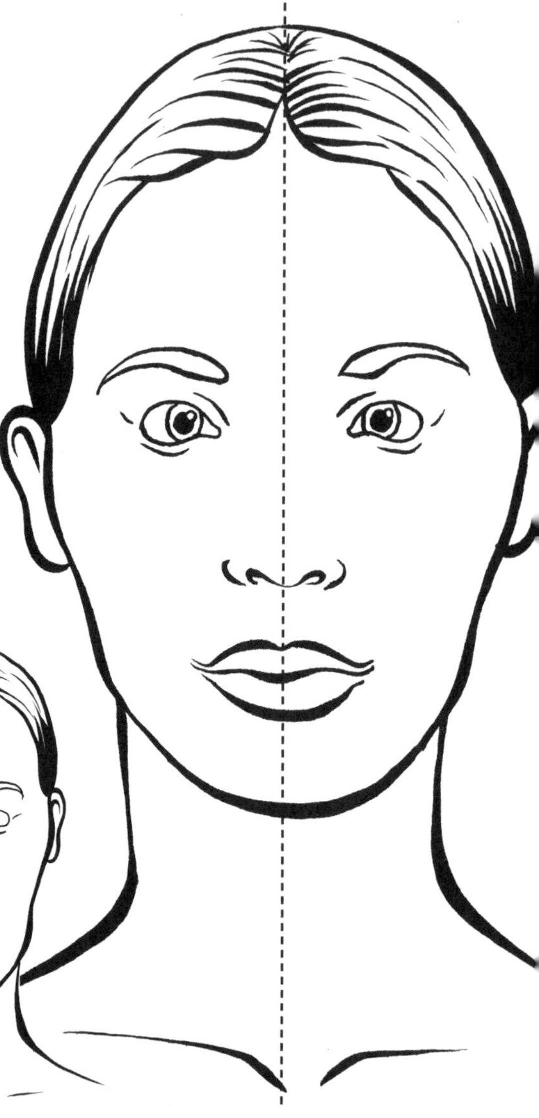

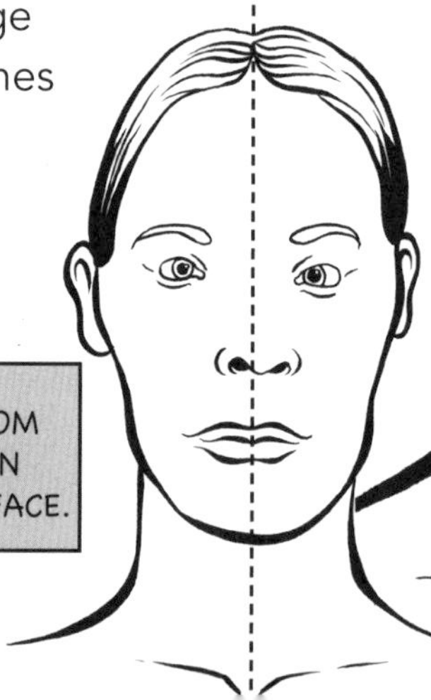

EVEN A SLIGHT DEVIATION FROM SYMMETRY AS SHOWN HERE CAN CHANGE HOW WE PERCEIVE A FACE.

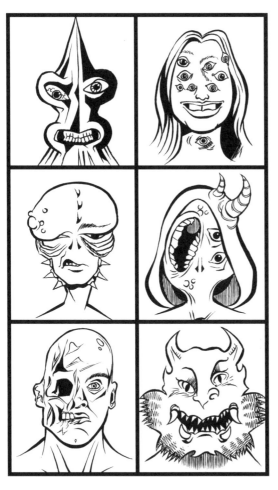

BIZARRE BEAUTY Pageant

Mirror, mirror, on the wall, who's the ugliest of them all? You decide. Look at the pictures of the monsters shown here. Then rate them on a scale of one to five, where one is the "prettiest" monster and five is a complete terror. Which facial features repulse you the most?

prettiest

1 2 3 4 5

ugliest

Killer LOOKS!

Scientific studies have shown that attractive people are perceived as being more intelligent and popular than those less attractive. They also have an easier time getting jobs and dates. In scientific circles, it's called the "halo effect" — good-looking people are seen as perfect little angels. But beware! Some serial killers have used their attractiveness to lure unsuspecting prey. They know they have looks … to DIE for!

TRUTH OR Scare

Joseph Merrick (1862–1890), the Elephant Man, had a head that measured 1 m (39 in.) around and enormous fleshy tumors all over his face. His right hand was as thick as an elephant's trunk, while his left arm was the size of a ten-year-old girl's. He could weep but could not smile.

His physical problems, however, didn't stop Merrick from leading an interesting life. He was a friend to Queen Victoria and wrote poetry and prose. Sadly, he died before he could fulfill his greatest desire: to find a blind woman who would love him.

IF LOOKS COULD KILL...

... **V**AMPIRES WOULD BE ON TOP OF THE FOOD CHAIN. INDEED, IN MODERN FICTION MANY VAMPIRES ARE DROP-DEAD GORGEOUS. TAKE THE CULLEN CLAN IN STEPHENIE MEYER'S BEST-SELLING BOOK *TWILIGHT*. ALL OF THEM ARE "DEVASTATINGLY, INHUMANLY BEAUTIFUL." TURNS OUT, THOUGH, THAT THE CULLENS ARE REAL SUCKERS WHEN IT COMES TO RELATIONSHIPS.

Vampires are immortal, shape-shifting predators that survive by feeding on the blood of the living. Neither dead nor alive, they are **THE UNDEAD** and stalk the Earth in search of prey. Do real vampires exist? Well, hold on to your necks, guys and ghouls, because you're about to enter a realm where reality and the supernatural collide.

Baited BREATH?

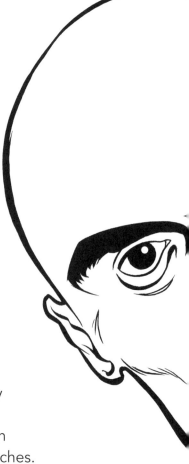

In Bram Stoker's 1897 classic vampire tale *Dracula*, Dr. Van Helsing protects Lucy from a vampire's bite by rubbing garlic all over her room and placing a wreath of it around her neck.

Scientists at the Scripps Research Institute in California and elsewhere have noted that raw garlic appears to be effective in keeping away mosquitoes and other bloodsucking insects, such as fleas and ticks. Garlic has an unusual number of complex sulfur-containing compounds, which give rise to the plant's pungent odor. This foul smell does not so much repel these tiny bloodsuckers as block their ability to detect what they do find appealing — blood!

Ah!, but beware: a study at the University of Bergen in Norway showed that garlic can *attract* bloodsucking leeches.

Vamps OR NO Vamps?

There is no such thing as a human vampire. But a group of rare blood diseases known as porphyria can cause symptoms that mimic those of a vampire.

If exposed to sunlight, the skin of a porphyria sufferer can burn, blister and scar. To avoid this reaction, the victims can go out only at night. The disease can turn the color of their urine and teeth red, leading to the misbelief that they drink blood. Sometimes their skin tightens and shrinks, causing their fingers, eyes and ears to appear deformed. This also makes their teeth more prominent, and their canine teeth look a bit like fangs.

While Stoker might have used the symptoms of porphyria to create his vampire, porphyria victims are not vampires. Casket closed!

FANGS of FEAR?

According to legend, vampires sometimes take the form of bats. Dracula's creator, Bram Stoker, recounts what happened to one young woman when Dracula went batty.

"One of those big bats that they call vampires had got at her in the night, and, what with his gorge and the vein left open, there wasn't enough blood in her to let her stand up ..."

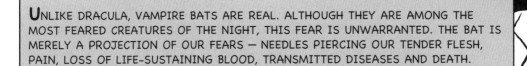

UNLIKE DRACULA, VAMPIRE BATS ARE REAL. ALTHOUGH THEY ARE AMONG THE MOST FEARED CREATURES OF THE NIGHT, THIS FEAR IS UNWARRANTED. THE BAT IS MERELY A PROJECTION OF OUR FEARS — NEEDLES PIERCING OUR TENDER FLESH, PAIN, LOSS OF LIFE-SUSTAINING BLOOD, TRANSMITTED DISEASES AND DEATH.

FREAKY FACTS

◊ Like some superheroes, vampire bats can leap into the air with a single bound.

◊ They prefer cattle blood and rarely nip humans. When they do it's usually on the toes, ears or nose.

◊ To find a juicy vein, they rely on heat sensors in their nose.

◊ The bat injects a chemical that numbs the skin so that the sleeping victim doesn't wake.

◊ The bat does not suck. It laps the flowing liquid with its tongue — about a tablespoonful in thirty minutes.

◊ A bat colony of about 100 can drink the blood of 25 cows in one year.

◊ Draculin, a blood-thinning drug developed from vampire bat saliva, helps prevent strokes and heart attacks in humans.

The worms crawl in, the worms crawl out,

The worms play pinochle on your snout.

They eat your eyes, they eat your nose,

They eat the jelly between your toes.

A great big worm with rolling eyes,

Crawls in your stomach and out your eyes.

Your stomach turns a slimy green,

And pus pours out like whipping cream.

You spread it on a slice of bread,

And that's what worms eat when

  you're dead.

— *From "The Hearse Song," author unknown*

Of **Corpse!**

The odor of decaying flesh attracts flies looking for a place to lay their eggs. Tiny white, wormlike maggots — definitely members of the love-blood club — emerge from these eggs and begin to feed on, and grow in, the decomposing flesh.

Maggots grow at constant rates, and scientists are using

that knowledge to their advantage. They can now examine maggots on a decomposing body, note their stage of development and determine how much time has passed since death occurred.

Blow flies are among the first to lay eggs on (or in) a corpse, usually within ten minutes of death, followed by flesh flies (not french fries!). The eggs of both, in turn, hatch into squirming maggots that morph into pupae. The pupae emerge from their shells as adult flies.

Entomologists (bug docs) know how long each stage takes under different conditions of humidity and temperature. Turns out the development is so predictable that courts allow maggots as evidence.

FREAKY FACTS

◆ Sterile maggots placed in a porous holder the size of a tea bag are now being used by doctors to clean severe wounds. The maggots eat only dead tissue. As they do so, they flood the wound with their own antibiotic secretions, which destroy bacteria. Maggots can trim dead flesh with more precision than scalpels. And their wriggling around on a wound may stimulate new tissue growth.

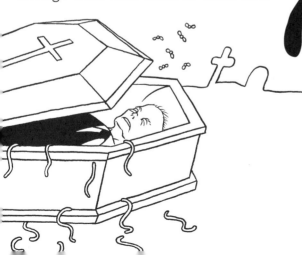

WEREWOLVES BITE!

Like vampires, werewolves were thought to be undead shape-shifters that fed on the blood of the living. And they could pass along the curse.

WHOEVER IS BITTEN BY A WEREWOLF AND LIVES WILL BECOME A WEREWOLF WHEN THE MOON IS BIG AND BRIGHT!

WEREWOLF LEGENDS FEED RIGHT INTO A COMMON CHILDHOOD FEAR OF ANIMALS, WHICH USUALLY DEVELOPS SOMETIME BETWEEN THE AGES OF THREE AND FIVE. IT'S A PROTECTIVE INSTINCT. CHILDREN MAY FEAR CERTAIN ANIMALS, ESPECIALLY IF THEY HAVE HAD A SCARY ENCOUNTER, LIKE BEING CHASED OR BITTEN. BUT MANY CHILDREN FEAR ANIMALS SIMPLY OUT OF A SENSE OF HELPLESSNESS. THE FEAR MAKES THEM WARY OF ANIMALS, WHICH HELPS TO KEEP THEM SAFE.

ABOUT AGE FIVE IS ALSO WHEN WE PICK UP ON OUR PARENTS' FEARS OF ANIMALS. LIKE BEING BITTEN BY A WEREWOLF, THESE FEARS CAN BE TRANSMITTED FROM GENERATION TO GENERATION — THE FEAR REMAINS "IN THE BLOOD."

Where did werewolves come from? One theory is that they were fictional manifestations of a human illness called clinical lycanthropy. It's a type of split-personality disorder that leads a person to believe that he or she has turned into a wolf and then act the part. Some sufferers might even have the urge to hunt down and eat live prey. Another theory points the finger at serial killers who lived centuries ago. Back then, people thought that only an animal would mutilate a human body with such savagery.

FREAKY FACTS

◗ Is *Little Red Riding Hood* a werewolf tale? Some scholars think so.

◗ People with the rare disease hypertrichosis sometimes have thick hair covering their entire bodies that makes them look like werewolves. The disease is believed to be a genetic disorder that affects only about one in 340 million people. That means fewer than twenty people alive today have the disease.

Bad MOON RISING?

Once bitten by a werewolf, you can expect to be transformed into a hairy beast on nights when the moon is full. Hey, everyone knows that the moon tugs on our brains and causes some people to flip out, right? Why, the words LUNACY and lunatic are derived from *luna*, Latin for moon. There's more crime on full-moon nights, more accidents, more suicides, more overall insanity, isn't there?

No. Most studies show no relationship between the phases of the moon and abnormal human behavior. However, one study *did* show that cases of aggravated assaults do occur more frequently during the full moon. Aha! Proof!

Not really. Just because these events occur together doesn't mean that one event causes the other. Maybe moonlight gives people a false sense of security, so they let their guard down and are more likely to be victimized. And maybe criminals, like wolves on the prowl, also realize the advantage of moonlight — "the better to see you with."

Death Becomes You!

The 1932 film *The Mummy* was the first movie to put the fear of gauze into us. In this tale of terror, a British archaeology team in Egypt finds a 4000-year-old embalmed corpse with a sacred scroll. When one of the scientists reads the scroll out loud, he accidentally revives the mummy, who steps out of his coffin — and straight into our nightmares.

Mummies cross the line from fantasy to reality. A mummy is, after all, the embalmed body of a dead person. We can see their wrapped remains in museums. They're real … and real dead.

When we see the mummy walk on the big screen, our belief that death is permanent vanishes — as does our sense of safety. And because mummies are wrapped from head to toe, we cannot see their faces or their expressions. DEATH, we see, has no face, and we fear that unknown.

A mummy that has returned to life has the power to take our breath away — maybe forever!

No Brainer!

THE ANCIENT EGYPTIANS BELIEVED THAT A PERSON'S BODY HAD TO BE PRESERVED SO THAT HE OR SHE COULD ENTER THE AFTERLIFE. THAT'S WHY THEY GOT SO WRAPPED UP IN MAKING MUMMIES. IN HIS 1845 SHORT STORY "SOME WORDS WITH A MUMMY," EDGAR ALLAN POE SUMMARIZES THE DRYING PROCESS:

THE BODY WAS THEN SHAVED, WASHED, AND SALTED...

THE BRAIN IT WAS CUSTOMARY TO WITHDRAW THROUGH THE NOSE...

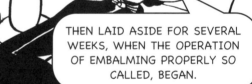

THEN LAID ASIDE FOR SEVERAL WEEKS, WHEN THE OPERATION OF EMBALMING PROPERLY SO CALLED, BEGAN.

THE INTESTINES THROUGH AN INCISION IN THE SIDE ...

THE HEART WAS THE ONLY ORGAN THAT REMAINED IN THE MUMMY'S BODY. THE LIVER, STOMACH, INTESTINES AND LUNGS WERE PRESERVED IN INDIVIDUAL CONTAINERS CALLED CANOPIC JARS AND PLACED IN THE TOMB WITH THE MUMMY. CONSIDERED UNIMPORTANT, THE BRAIN WAS TOSSED AWAY.

FREAKY FACTS

How did the ancient Egyptians pull a brain out of a nose? The Greek historian Herodotus, who visited Egypt around 450 BC, reported that they first poked a hole in the thin ethmoid bone at the top of the nostrils. They then inserted a large bronze needle with a hooked or spiral end and pulled the brain out in pieces.

The Last Mumzy?

In 1994, scientists from the University of Maryland and Long Island University made the first human mummy in nearly 2000 years.

Before he died from heart failure, an elderly man from Baltimore, Maryland, donated his body to the project. The scientists had ancient Egyptian embalming tools manufactured. They then traveled to Egypt and brought back 91 m (300 ft.) of fine linen and more than 275 kg (600 lbs.) of natron, a chemical the Egyptians used to dry the body.

Following Herodotus's ancient account, the scientists then began a roughly month-long drying, embalming and wrapping process. It was a complete success! The scientists say the MUMMIFIED body is not destined for the afterlife. Instead, it is resting in the Museum of Man in San Diego, California, where its longevity will be studied.

Death Wishes ... from Mum!

Mummies were buried with many possessions deemed necessary in the afterlife — including gold and other jewels, things that grave robbers adore. To scare off trespassers, some tombs had curses written on them.

"They who enter this sacred tomb shall swift be visited by wings of death." This horrifying curse was supposedly written in hieroglyphs at the entrance of King Tutankhamen's tomb.

Shockingly, on April 5, 1923, seven weeks after entering the king's burial chamber, Lord Carnarvon, who had funded the discovery of the tomb, died. At that same moment, his dog died, too. And all the lights went out in nearby Cairo, Egypt.

Sir Arthur Conan Doyle, author of the Sherlock Holmes mysteries, announced that Carnarvon's death could have been the result of a "Pharaoh's Curse." Within a decade, the press had linked more than thirty deaths to Tutankhamen's curse.

That's a WRAP!

Was Tut's tomb really cursed?

Eighty years after Lord Carnarvon's death, Mark Nelson, an Australian epidemic disease specialist, decided to find out. He traced thirty-six people associated with Lord Carnarvon's expedition. Some of them had been exposed to Tut's tomb — they had either entered it or were present for a major event associated with it. The others had nothing to do with the tomb. Here's what Nelson found:

• All of the people enjoyed a relatively long life.

• The people who were present at the tomb lived to an average age of seventy years.

• The people who were not exposed to the tomb lived to an average age of seventy-five years.

Maybe one could argue that the curse sucked some breath out of the exposed group — so that they lost, on average, five years of their lives. Unfortunately, that argument holds about as much weight as a mummy's ghost. You see, most of the people in the unexposed group were women. And women live, on average, about seven years longer than men.

Bottom line: Nelson found no evidence that being exposed to King Tut's tomb shortened a person's life.

Curses! Coffin closed.

BREATH OF Death

"Anyone who disturbs these tombs, I will ring his neck like a bird."

That's a real curse from a real Egyptian tomb. Lately scientists have begun to wonder if there isn't some truth to this and other **CURSES** that appear on tombs. But maybe it's not the curse that's deadly, rather something inside the tombs.

In 1999, German microbiologist Gotthard Kramer decided to find out. He analyzed forty mummies and identified several potentially deadly mold spores on each one.

THESE SPORES MIGHT BE ABLE TO SURVIVE FOR THOUSANDS OF YEARS IN A SEALED TOMB.

BREAK THE TOMB'S SEAL AND A FLOW OF FRESH AIR COULD RELEASE THE SPORES INTO THE AIR WHERE THEY COULD BE INHALED.

IF THE SPORES ENTER THE BODY THROUGH THE MUCOUS MEMBRANES OF THE NOSE, MOUTH OR EYE, THEY MIGHT LEAD TO ORGAN FAILURE OR EVEN DEATH, KRAMER SAYS.

DEADLY SPORES MAY HAVE KILLED SCIENTISTS AND GRAVE ROBBERS IN THE PAST. WHO KNOWS WHAT HORRORS OTHER SPORES HAVE IN STORE FOR TOMB RAIDERS IN THE FUTURE?

MUMMY MURDER Mystery

WHILE PERFORMING THE CT SCAN OF KING TUT, THE RESEARCHERS NOTED SEVERAL STRANGE EVENTS: THE ELECTRICITY SUDDENLY BLINKED OUT. THE CT SCANNER COULD NOT BE STARTED. AND ONE TEAM MEMBER FELL ILL. COINCIDENCE? OR WAS IT THE PHARAOH'S CURSE? HMMM …

X-rays of King Tut's mummified body taken in 1968 revealed bone fragments inside his skull. The bone bits suggested Tut might have been murdered 3300 years ago, perhaps killed by a blow to the back of the head.

But a new 3-D image made in 2005 from a CT scan of the mummy found no evidence of a skull fracture. The loose bone pieces in the skull probably originated from a mishap during mummification. They are likely to be bits of backbone, not skull.

What, then, is the official cause of DEATH? Ashraf Selim of Cairo University in Egypt says that Tut had a badly broken leg that became infected.

FIRST-PERSON ACCOUNT: A REAL UFO!

One night, at Harvard College Observatory near Boston, I was tracking what I thought was a satellite through a small telescope attached to a big one. When a colleague looked at the magnified image through the large telescope, he screamed, "I don't believe it!"

Just then, the satellite made a sharp ninety-degree turn. (Satellites don't do that!) Quickly, I switched places with my friend and saw — with disbelief — the ghostly white form of a flying saucer with winglike extensions. After looping across the sky it receded and vanished! My colleague and I immediately made drawings of what we saw and then compared them. They were identical!

LOOK! WE BOTH SAW A SAUCER! A FLYING SAUCER.

NO. WE SAW AN UNIDENTIFIED FLYING OBJECT.

STILL, MY HEART RACED. DID I SEE A REAL FLYING SAUCER? I DECIDED NOT TO FILL OUT AN UNIDENTIFIED FLYING OBJECT (UFO) REPORT. MY TRAINING AS A SCIENTIST TOLD ME TO EVALUATE THE SIGHTING CAREFULLY BEFORE MAKING A CLAIM. AMAZINGLY, THE MYSTERIOUS OBJECT APPEARED AGAIN THE NEXT EVENING. FIRST IT WHISKED ACROSS THE NORTHERN HORIZON — BEFORE IT FLEW JUST A FEW YARDS ABOVE MY HEAD. IT WAS THEN THAT I REALIZED MY UFO WAS ACTUALLY AN OWL, WHOSE OVAL BELLY AND WINGS WERE BEING ILLUMINATED BY THE CITY LIGHTS.

Do **UFOs** Exist?

Absolutely! UFOs are flying objects you cannot identify. That doesn't mean they are from another planet.

It's fun to scare yourself silly at the thought of alien life forms visiting Earth. But here are some facts you need to know:

• The U.S. National Academy of Sciences (NAS) — "advisers to the nation on science, engineering, and medicine" — has never clearly identified any debris as coming from a crashed extraterrestrial spacecraft.

• The NAS has never seen other evidence that conclusively proves that the Earth has been visited by extraterrestrial spacecraft.

> **I**S IT POSSIBLE THAT SOME DAY OUR PLANET WILL BE VISITED BY AN EXTRATERRESTRIAL SPACESHIP. YES. IS IT LIKELY? READ ON!

Are We Alone?

Our galaxy, the Milky Way, is a big place. It is home to about 400 billion stars, spread over a huge area. Scientists calculate that about half of those stars have planets and that half of those planets might have life. But — and this is the big question — how many of those planets have intelligent life, intelligent enough to communicate with us?

The answer is, no one knows. Some scientists estimate there are about fifty intelligent civilizations that could, at this very moment, be trying to make contact with us! Are you listening?

Some people believe that contact with extraterrestrials (ETs) has already been made. Extraordinary tales abound of ETs kidnapping human beings and subjecting them to terrifying genetic experiments.

The problem is that only people who already believed in UFOs claim to have been **ABDUCTED** … no skeptics have. And that's not all. Some UFO abductees have admitted to making up their stories to get attention. Others have confessed to creating these fantasies to voice their concerns about the fate of humankind.

MARTIAN INVADERS?

Do Martians exist? Mars is smaller than Earth and farther away from the Sun, so it could have cooled to the right temperature for life before Earth did. And chunks of rock blasting from Mars have been known to fall to Earth. Some scientists wonder if a Martian rock teeming with microscopic life could have landed on our primitive planet and helped to kick-start life here. More complex life forms could have developed from these microscopic Martian organisms. To see a Martian, then, maybe you need only to look in a mirror!

Got Flesh?

FREAKY FACTS

No bones about it — skeletons are the ultimate symbol of death. Their images have been carved on gravestones at least since the Middle Ages. Some tombstones show skeletons snuffing out candles (life is over) or attacking a person with an arrow (sudden death). Others show them with Father Time (time's up!). And when death comes knocking, it's the Grim Reaper, a hooded skeleton carrying a scythe (time to harvest the soul).

Despite their connection with death, skeletons are very popular. They appear in horror tales and movies, such as *Pirates of the Caribbean* and *Corpse Bride*. Curiously, true encounters with walking, talking, flying or SCREAMING skeletons are extremely rare. Where have all the skeletons gone?

◆ Why do animated skeletons frighten us? Perhaps because they have no minds, yet they think. They have no eyes, but they see. They have no muscles, yet they walk. Now here's the really scary part — animated skeletons do exist. As anyone who has ever had an X-ray knows … the terror is within you!

◆ Skeletons are the structural foundation of our bodies. You couldn't walk without one. Maybe that's why we shudder at seeing someone who is extremely thin — they look like a "walking skeleton."

The Forgotten Prisoner

Want to scare yourself to death? Look at this image, called "The Forgotten Prisoner of Castel-Maré." The original artwork appeared on the box of a 1966 Aurora model kit of the same name.

The prisoner is a skeleton in tattered clothes, chained by the neck and leg to a **DUNGEON** wall. Did he die screaming in helpless agony, knowing full well that no one would ever hear him, no one would ever come for him … except Death? The image combines our fear of skeletons (death) with the greatest childhood fear — abandonment.

The skeleton has no identity, no history, no personal connection. It's just a bunch of bones forgotten by all, doomed to decay alone — as if that person never existed.

The Forgotten Prisoner ... for Real?

A prominent Roman lawyer, Pliny the Younger, who was born about 61 AD, wrote a letter to a Roman senator asking him if he believed in ghosts. Pliny then went on to share a "remarkable" and "terrifying" story of a haunted house in Athens rented by the philosopher Athenodorus. Here are the highlights of that story.

In the dead of night, Athenodorus heard the clanking of iron and the rattle of chains. Suddenly the specter of an old man appeared, wearing fetters on his legs and shaking the chains on his wrists. The ghost stood and beckoned, as if summoning Athenodorus, who picked up his lamp and followed. The specter moved slowly, and when it turned off into the courtyard of the house, it suddenly VANISHED.

ATHENODORUS MARKED THE SPOT AND HAD IT DUG UP THE NEXT DAY. "THERE THEY FOUND BONES," PLINY SAID, "TWISTED ROUND WITH CHAIN ..."

DON'T FEAR THE REAPER!

Feeling haunted by death? Lady Grace Gethin, an English noblewoman who lived in the late 1600s, gave this advice:

"Nothing is worse for one's health than to be in fear of death. Think of it as little as possible."

You could also do what people in Mexico and Latin America do to ease their minds about death. Every November 1st and 2nd, they celebrate death! Their *Días de los Muertos* (Days of the Dead) is a holiday that is a cross between Halloween and Mardi Gras. People decorate graves and have boneyard picnics. They light fireworks, make candy skulls and dress up

papier-mâché or wooden skeletons as if they were alive and going about their business. Seeing skeletons "kicking up their heels" spawns levity and that invites longevity. Laughter really is the best medicine for postponing your appointment with **DEATH**.

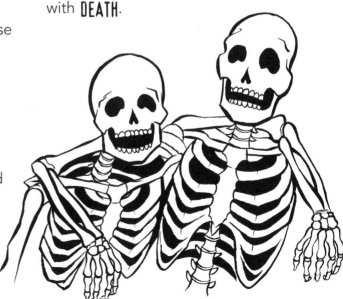

A FIRST-PERSON ACCOUNT: A GHOST Story!

DO YOU BELIEVE IN GHOSTS? WELL, GATHER ROUND, BECAUSE I'M GOING TO TELL YOU MY OWN PERSONAL TALE OF TERROR. THE STORY TAKES PLACE AT HARVARD COLLEGE OBSERVATORY, WHICH HAS BEEN THE SITE OF SEVERAL HAUNTINGS.

I WANTED TO FIND THE DIARY OF THE OBSERVATORY'S SECOND DIRECTOR, GEORGE PHILLIPS BOND, WHO DIED NEAR THIS SPOT IN 1865.

IN THE DEEP QUIET OF THE NIGHT, I BEGAN TO FEEL UNCOMFORTABLE. I FELT LIKE SOMEONE WAS STANDING RIGHT BEHIND ME, LOOKING OVER MY SHOULDER.

ONE EVENING AFTER THE STROKE OF MIDNIGHT, I WAS IN THE LIBRARY ALONE, SEARCHING THROUGH STACKS OF OLD BOOKS.

I TURNED AROUND, BUT NO ONE WAS THERE. STILL, I COULD NOT SHAKE THE FEELING OF A PRESENCE.

WHEN I FINALLY FOUND THE BOOK, I BENT OVER TO PICK IT UP. SUDDENLY I FELT A COLD FINGER RUNNING UP MY SPINE.

LEAPING IN FRIGHT, I SAW, STANDING BUT A FEW FEET IN FRONT OF ME, THE GHOSTLY FORM OF HALF A MAN — SLICED VERTICALLY FROM HEAD TO TOE.

THE GHOST DID NOT SPEAK, NOR DID IT MOVE. IT REMAINED VISIBLE FOR A FEW SECONDS, THEN VANISHED.

I COULD SEE ONLY HIS LEFT SIDE. THE MAN HAD THIN, WAVY HAIR AND WAS DRESSED IN A FORMAL TAILCOAT. ON HIS BREAST WAS A SILVER MEDAL — THE ONLY COLOR TO BE SEEN.

DID I SEE THE GHOST OF A CENTURIES-OLD ASTRONOMER? OR CAN SCIENCE EXPLAIN THIS MYSTERIOUS VISITOR? READ ON.

GHOSTS IN Limb-O

Many people claim to have seen ghosts that emerge like holograms from thin air.

Peter Brugger, a neuroscientist at University Hospital in Zürich, Switzerland, believes that ghosts are "phantom images" created and projected by the human mind. He says they are mental sensations caused by neurons firing on a whim.

Some people who have had an arm or a leg amputated still sense the presence of these lost limbs. Ghosts, Brugger believes, are similar sensations, but expanded to the whole body.

WAS THE HARVARD GHOST A PRODUCT OF MY OWN BRAIN? WELL, I AGREE THAT THE MIND CAN CREATE ILLUSIONS. BUT, HAVING ACTUALLY SEEN A GHOST, I AM ALSO OPEN TO OTHER EXPLANATIONS. DO I BELIEVE THAT THE GHOST I SAW WAS THE SPIRIT OF A DEAD PERSON MADE VISIBLE TO ME? I DO NOT HAVE THE ANSWER.

FREAKY FACTS

◊ Is there life after death? No one knows. Certainly anyone who says there's not is a liar. Why? Because you'd have to die to know the answer.

◊ Lack of oxygen to the brain's temporal lobe can cause hallucinations. As evidence, neuroscientist Peter Brugger tells of eight mountaineers who had climbed above 8200 m (27 000 ft.) without the aid of oxygen. They reported feeling a phantom presence and had out-of-body experiences.

◊ A few months after Brutus stabbed Julius Caesar to death on March 15, 44 BC, grieving crowds saw Caesar's ghost rising in the sky over Rome. Now we know that the apparition was a rare daytime comet.

Are You **Out** of Your **Mind?**

MOST PEOPLE FEAR DEATH, BUT, SURPRISINGLY, NOT PEOPLE WHO HAVE ACTUALLY DIED. MILLIONS OF PEOPLE HAVE HAD NEAR-DEATH EXPERIENCES (NDEs) — THE EXPERIENCE OF BEING CLINICALLY DEAD AND THEN RETURNING TO LIFE. THEY SAY THEY FELT PEACE, NOT FEAR, AS THEY "DIED." ONE PERSON I KNOW SAID IT WAS THE MOST PEACEFUL SHE'S EVER FELT.

MOST PEOPLE SAY THEY TRAVEL THROUGH A TUNNEL TOWARD A BRIGHT LIGHT.

SOME SEE FRIENDLY FORMS OF LIGHT ENERGY. OTHERS MEET DECEASED RELATIVES AND FRIENDS.

DURING THIS MYSTERIOUS JOURNEY, MANY PEOPLE HAVE FLASHBACKS AND RELIVE SOME IMPORTANT OR BEAUTIFUL MOMENTS IN THEIR LIVES.

OTHERS SAY THEY CAN SEE WHAT'S HAPPENING AROUND THEM, AS IF THEY WERE OUTSIDE THEIR BODIES.

Back from the Dead

Are NDEs real? Absolutely! Do people really come back from the dead? Well, they come back from clinical death — the moment when a person's heart stops beating and their breathing stops. A person can be in this state for about five minutes and still be revived.

Science may be able to explain some NDEs:

• Feeling at peace is probably due to endorphins. The brain releases these chemicals to calm the body during trauma.

• The dark tunnel may be the eyes "blacking out" due to a lack of oxygen. As oxygen returns to the eyes, the reviving patient would see a light that grows increasingly larger, creating an illusion of movement toward it.

• The brain might also confuse incoming information about where the body is in relation to the space around it, creating an out-of-body experience.

The biggest problem with NDEs is that there is no way to prove them or test what's happening during them, because you can't repeat the "experiment." Well, at least no one is dying to.

IMAGINE WE ARE STANDING ON THE FRONT PORCH OF A CREEPY OLD HOUSE WITH BROKEN WINDOWS AND PEELING PAINT. INSIDE, WE'RE TOLD, WALKS THE RESTLESS SPIRIT OF A WOMAN WHO WAS MURDERED THERE A HUNDRED YEARS AGO.

COME NOW AND PUSH OPEN THE OAK DOOR. DON'T WORRY ABOUT THE CREAKING HINGES — YOU ARE THE FIRST PERSON TO ENTER IN MORE THAN FIFTY YEARS. (THE LAST PERSON WAS NEVER HEARD FROM AGAIN.) STEP RIGHT IN TO THE FOYER. DO YOU FEEL A CHILL RUNNING UP YOUR SPINE? IF SO, YOU MIGHT HAVE WALKED RIGHT INTO A COLD SPOT — THE MOURNFUL HEART OF THE HAUNTED HOUSE.

Chill Out!

A "cold spot" is one of the supposed signs that a ghost is present. The theory behind cold spots is that ghosts need to draw heat energy to become visible.

Many cold spots in old houses have a natural source, such as a drafty window, chimney or broken floorboard. But Richard Wiseman of the University of Hertfordshire discovered that a cold sensation can also come from reduced humidity. He found that some locations reported to be haunted were significantly less humid than those that were not.

FREAKY FACTS

◊ How cold we feel is not an exact science. Studies have shown that, if we are told that something is unpleasantly cold, we'll feel colder — ghost or no ghost.

Scary House

It's easy to imagine that old, rotting houses are haunted, maybe because they are wooden corpses of homes that were once filled with life. Or maybe we get caught up in the haunting legends associated with some places and want to believe in them.

By definition, a haunted house is a dwelling inhabited by a ghost or ghosts and plagued by ghostly occurrences, events that lead us to question the laws of science — and sometimes our own sanity. It's fun to leave your brain at the doorstep of a supposed haunted house and scare yourself silly. It's also easy to imagine creaking floorboards as ghostly footsteps or to feel a rush of wind as icy fingers on your neck. But are some houses really haunted?

The HAUNTED Mind

Canadian neuroscientist Michael Persinger believes that hauntings are real but ghosts are not.

To prove it, Persinger had volunteers wear a special helmet that generated a weak electromagnetic wave pattern. The electrical activity caused "mini-seizures" in the brain's temporal lobes, which are involved in processing what we see and hear. His test subjects sensed a supernatural presence in the room and had other paranormal experiences. Ghosts may live in a haunted dwelling after all — our heads!

Now for the spooky part! In some "haunted" places, researchers have measured strong magnetic fields that fluctuate wildly. These fluctuations may interact with the brain, causing hallucinations, dizziness or other mind tricks that can make a person feel as if a house has "a presence." What causes these mind-altering local magnetic fluctuations? Skeptics say it could be anything from magnetic minerals in the ground to sunspots. But believers will tell you ghosts are the cause. One thing is certain, until scientists can solve this mystery, believers won't give up the ghost.

Bad Vibes!

If an angry old house could talk, it might sound like the one in Yorkshire, England, that mystified skeptical investigators in the 1950s. For months the house, which was built about 100 m (330 ft.) from a river, shook with explosive sounds, like doors slamming. But as Christopher Maynard explains in his book *Mysteries of the Unknown*, the haunting presence behind the sounds turned out to be high tides forcing water up into an old forgotten sewer filled with soil.

As the tides rose and fell, so did the water in the sewer. And when the water seeped from the sewer into the soil under the house's foundation, it caused the foundation to shift and the house to shudder and shake. Indeed, the investigators discovered that the ghostly noises rose and fell with the rhythm of the tides.

FREAKY FACTS

◊ Banging noises are common in haunted houses. Many of them have been explained by natural causes. Trapped air in a radiator, for instance, can create ghostly knocking and rapping sounds. And if the flow of water in a pipe is quickly shut off, a shock wave can move down the pipe and create a rumbling or shaking vibration. So the next time you hear a strange knocking in your house, don't call Ghost Busters, call the plumbers!

SHIVER ME TIMBERS

Old houses are notorious "chatterboxes." They react to changes in atmospheric pressure, temperature, moisture and humidity. Any movement of materials, no matter how slight, can create a mysterious noise. A creaking floorboard, for example, might be caused by a sudden change in temperature. The nails in the floorboard expand (when hot) or contract (when cold) at a rate that's different from the surrounding wood. The result: a ghostly footstep.

Experiments have also shown that infrasound — low-frequency sound waves inaudible to humans — can cause "ghostly" phenomena. These include shivers up the spine, feelings of nervousness and discomfort, as well as a sense of a presence in the room.

Infrasound may also make the human eye vibrate, making people see things that aren't there.

Spooky stuff!

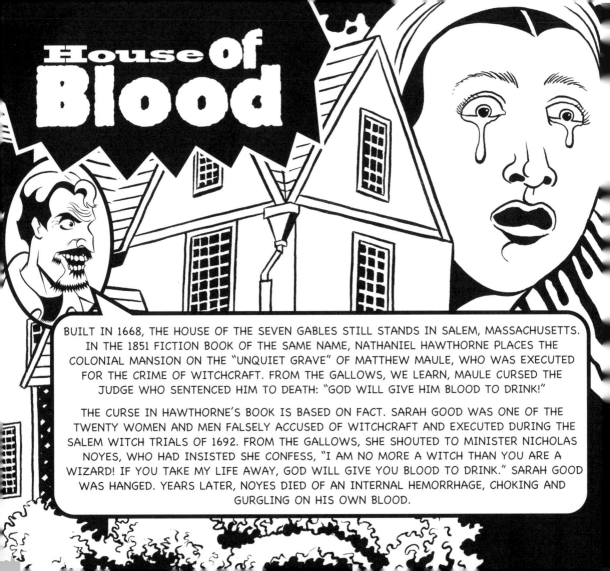

House Of Blood

BUILT IN 1668, THE HOUSE OF THE SEVEN GABLES STILL STANDS IN SALEM, MASSACHUSETTS. IN THE 1851 FICTION BOOK OF THE SAME NAME, NATHANIEL HAWTHORNE PLACES THE COLONIAL MANSION ON THE "UNQUIET GRAVE" OF MATTHEW MAULE, WHO WAS EXECUTED FOR THE CRIME OF WITCHCRAFT. FROM THE GALLOWS, WE LEARN, MAULE CURSED THE JUDGE WHO SENTENCED HIM TO DEATH: "GOD WILL GIVE HIM BLOOD TO DRINK!"

THE CURSE IN HAWTHORNE'S BOOK IS BASED ON FACT. SARAH GOOD WAS ONE OF THE TWENTY WOMEN AND MEN FALSELY ACCUSED OF WITCHCRAFT AND EXECUTED DURING THE SALEM WITCH TRIALS OF 1692. FROM THE GALLOWS, SHE SHOUTED TO MINISTER NICHOLAS NOYES, WHO HAD INSISTED SHE CONFESS, "I AM NO MORE A WITCH THAN YOU ARE A WIZARD! IF YOU TAKE MY LIFE AWAY, GOD WILL GIVE YOU BLOOD TO DRINK." SARAH GOOD WAS HANGED. YEARS LATER, NOYES DIED OF AN INTERNAL HEMORRHAGE, CHOKING AND GURGLING ON HIS OWN BLOOD.

Fraidy Cat!

Do you believe that black cats bring bad luck? Black cats got their bad reps because they were thought to be witches in disguise.

Well, fear no more. Stephen O'Brien and Eduardo Eizirik of the U.S. National Cancer Institute in Maryland have found that black cats are, in fact, quite lucky. The gene that gives a cat its black coat (called MC1R) may also provide the animal with a resistance to disease. Since humans have a similar gene, scientists may soon learn how to boost human resistance to deadly diseases like AIDS. Talk about black magic!

THE SOUND OF HORROR

When a scream breaks the stillness of the night, our fear response immediately goes into high gear — even though there may be no immediate danger. No one knows why hearing someone scream gives us the shivers, but you can bet it has something to do with past experience and our instinct to survive. Usually, people don't scream unless they're afraid. Hearing someone scream warns us that something's up, and we'd better pay attention.

Loud noises are one of our earliest childhood fears. Even infants react to them. And though that fear usually lessens with time, researchers have found that it can quickly return in new ways. In laboratory tests, for instance, researchers played a loud noise to those who feared loud noises. At the same time, they flashed a light. The test subjects quickly learned to fear flashing lights — even without the loud noise. So if we hear a scream coming from a creepy old house, we may fear creepy old houses in the future — just by sight alone.

Scream, Silly!

Screaming is a good remedy for fear, especially during horror movies or other safe but frightening activities, such as taking a roller coaster ride. Screaming gives us a sense of conquering something that seems threatening, and we end up feeling better. When someone sneaks up on us and shouts, "Boo!" we jump and scream … until we realize there is no harm. Then we laugh ourselves to (ahem!) death.

A MOMENT OF
Silence?

What's the most frightening sound of all? How about complete silence. Why? Because it reminds us of the grave. Complete silence only comes to you when you're dead. Boo!

WELL, FIENDS, IT'S BEEN A SCREAM. BUT IT LOOKS LIKE THE SAND IN OUR HOURGLASS HAS RUN OUT. IT'S TIME TO RING THE BELL, CLOSE THE BOOK AND QUENCH THE CANDLE. I WISH YOU WELL IN YOUR CONTINUING EXPLORATIONS OF THE UNKNOWN. WITHOUT EXPLORATION, THERE IS NO KNOWLEDGE. SO KEEP AN OPEN MIND — JUST NOT SO OPEN THAT ZOMBIES CAN GET IN THERE AND DEVOUR YOUR BRAIN.

"The most beautiful experience we can have

is the mysterious ...

Whoever does not know it and can no longer wonder,

no longer marvel, is as good as **DEAD** ..."

— Albert Einstein

STOP! DEAD END!